The Ca alignme

Neolithic temples

Jean-Pierre Mohen
conservateur général du patrimoine

The Carnac alignments are one of the most spectacular and most intriguing monumental series of megaliths in the world. Erected 6 000 years ago, three thousand monoliths have been part of the Breton landscape since prehistoric times. Over the centuries the site has given rise to many legends, representing attempts to understand and explain its origins in the light of folklore and the Scriptures. The myths concerning Carnac may today make us smile or arouse passions, but they do not allow us to comprehend the builders' intentions.

In the mid-19th century a new era began when Jacques Boucher de Perthes "invented" prehistory by demonstrating that Man had appeared at a much earlier date than previously believed. Observations and archaeological investigations have continued ever since and their results are beginning to provide some answers. Although they are now better known, the Carnac alignments – and the Neolithic population who erected them and used them between the 5th and the first half of the 3rd

millennium BC – are far from having surrendered all their secrets. This aura of mystery surrounding the three great menhir systems – Kerlescan, Kermario and Le Ménec – fascinates visitors who, in order truly to discover the alignments, have to assimilate their exceptional scale.

The legend of St Cornelius

During the 1950s and 1960s children still chanted the legend of the menhirs♦ as follows: "All these stones were once upon a time an ancient Gaulish cemetery. For each dead person a stone was raised; if it was someone rich it was a large stone, if someone poor, a small one…".

Another legend, transmitted by a long tradition going back to the 18th century, tells of St Cornelius, who became pope in the 3rd century: the saint "pursued to the very seashore by pagan soldiers, and finding no boat to flee, turned around and changed all the soldiers into stones". One version of this legend tells how the saint hid in an ox's ear; to thank the animal for saving him from the Roman soldiers he was said to have instituted an ox cult. The church at Carnac, dedicated to him in 1639, and several other churches in the Morbihan own carved images of St Cornelius accompanied by his oxen.

Was an ox (or bull) cult associated with the megalithic site? A few disconcerting discoveries could point to this, in particular two bulls with long lyre-shaped horns picked into the capstone of the Gavrinis passage tomb. The ox or bull does indeed symbolise

♦**Menhir:**
A standing stone. The late 18th-century "Celtomaniacs" imposed the word "menhir" or "minhir" to designate a tall upright stone. Dom Grégoire de Rostrenen published a dictionary in 1732 which, for the word pillar, gives the equivalents peulvan (stone pillar in Breton), men hir and men sao (standing stones). Menhirs may be single and isolated or form alignments or enclosures.

St Cornelius' long-horned ox, on the church door at Malestroit (Morbihan).

the masculine component of rural fertility, and occupied an essential position alongside the mother-goddess in the Neolithic religions of the Near East, Central Europe and the Mediterranean region.

However the uninterrupted handing down of the cult for 6 000 years until the contemporary period and how it was Christianised have not been satisfactorily demonstrated.

St Cornelius, on the front of the church at Carnac, blessing the faithful, flanked by his two oxen, with the alignments in the background.

The long-horned ox pecked on one of the roof slabs at Gavrinis originally (circa 4300 BC) decorated a giant menhir at Locmariaquer. Was megalithic power, in particular that of the standing stones, compared, even during Neolithic times, with bovine strength?

Folklore

The Carnac alignments◆ inspire imagination. Among the legends collected in the early 20th century by the archaeologist Zacharie Le Rouzic, several present the monoliths either as living beings or as stones guarding a secret – treasure hidden under their base, for example – the disclosure of which would result in death.

In a collection of tales from the region of Carnac published in 1909, Le Rouzic records: "One day old Galudec, called Moh tu, threw down one of the large stones from the top of Le Ménec to seek the treasure; but when the stone fell, the treasure had flown!". Further on, Le Rouzic evokes the particularly tall menhir of Krifol, called Minour Krifol, located to the north of the Ménec system: it was said to be a young man changed into stone. A very

8 | *Below*

The Carnac menhirs go to drink, one night a year, on Christmas Eve. Engraving by Méaulle after Chiflar.

The Le Ménec alignments; this illustration, rarely for the 19th century, insists on their parallelism and shows their semicircular enclosure in the foreground.

rich only son, he was said to have spent all his inheritance on foolish things, so God changed him into a menhir, condemning his soul to remain with the stone. The young man's groans were long said to be heard around Mânni Krifol. According to one version, Minour Krifol was betrothed to a rich heiress, terrified to discover he turned into a menhir at night. In other versions, one of the soldiers chasing St Cornelius is said to have tarried in the village of Kerlann to drink some milk; before he could join his companions, he was turned to stone by the saint.

The mythical figures who haunt the megaliths could also appear as fairies or dwarfs, called goblins ("kerrions" or "korrigans" in Breton). These goblins live in the hollows of rocks and dolmens, which they are said to be strong enough to move. Their magical powers manifest themselves on the Sabbath.

This folklore bears witness to the desire to provide some explanation for these standing stones, "anomalies" of Nature which could not at the time be conceived of as having a human origin. These "phenomena", felt to be the

bearers of some message, were associated with the invisible, the uncanny, the sacred. The interest and respect they inspired helped preserve the megaliths.

There is, however, more to it: after centuries of blind groping, science now confirms that the intuition responsible for such interpretations was well-founded.

Caesar's army turned to stone, an interpretation of the Le Ménec lines. Wash drawing by F. Debret, early 19th century (Paris, Bibliothèque des Arts Décoratifs).

The size of the menhirs is exaggerated, frontispiece of *Essai sur des monuments armoricains [...]* by Comte Maudet de Penhouët, 1805.

Scholarly interest in the menhirs

Marquis de Robien, after the frontispiece of his ms. *Description historique, topographique et naturelle de l'ancienne Armorique,* 1756 (Rennes, municipal library).

The rows of menhirs began to attract the attention of scholars around the mid-18th century. Marquis Paul Christophe de Robien, a president of the Parliament of Brittany, made the first drawing of the Kermario standing stones. He proposed the hypothesis that they were funerary stelae but also inclined towards the idea of F.-F. Royer de La Sauvagère, the king's head engineer at Port-Louis, for whom the alignments were the remains of Caesar's camp when he came to conquer the Veneti during the Gallic Wars. La Sauvagère drew up a plan on which each row of menhirs is separated from the next by a fairly regular space varying between six fathoms and three fathoms three feet (a fathom, the old French unit of measurement the *toise*, is equal to six feet, i.e. almost two metres); within each row, the distance between the stones is eighteen, twenty or twenty-five feet. The engineer had also counted the megaliths – over four thousand! – and tried to estimate their weight: "I have gauged some which must exceed 80 thousand-weight [i.e. 80 tonnes]", he wrote. In his publication of 1805 about the celtic world, Jacques de Cambry had himself illustrated directing a small team of surveyors measuring the standing stones. This print, which shows the menhirs on an exaggeratedly large scale, induces some scepticism as to the use Cambry made of his data. A sense of measurement did however gradually assert itself and in 1832 the English geometer Vicars made the first correct plan of Carnac.

Right-hand page **And yet they were measured!** Print from *Monumens [sic] celtiques, ou Recherches sur le culte des pierres* by Jacques de Cambry, 1805.

The scientific approach advocated by Prosper Mérimée was set in place between 1864 and 1872 when the Englishmen W. C. Lukis and Sir H. Dryden began drawing up accurate plans of the Carnac alignments,

indicating their measurement figures. These plans are all the more precious in that they were made before certain stones, recumbent at the time, were raised. These documents are archived in Guernsey, London and Oxford. In 1873 Henri du Cleuziou was given an official mission. He made numerous drawings, bird's-eye views and cross-sections of Carnac, from which he established an aerial projection of the Kerlescan site, published in 1887 in *La Création de l'homme et les premiers âges de l'humanité [The Creation of Man and the First Ages of Humanity]*, one of the first books of scientific popularisation of the subject. In it, the notion of space is meticulously rendered. This notion was also explored by Commandant A. Devoir from the point of view of solar orientation, in particular that of the

Plan et Vue de XI Allignemens de 370 Pierres qui se
Avec les distances qui

PL. CXXI

Largeur totale de 47 toises

Plan general du Monument de 765.

T. VI

Côté de Carna

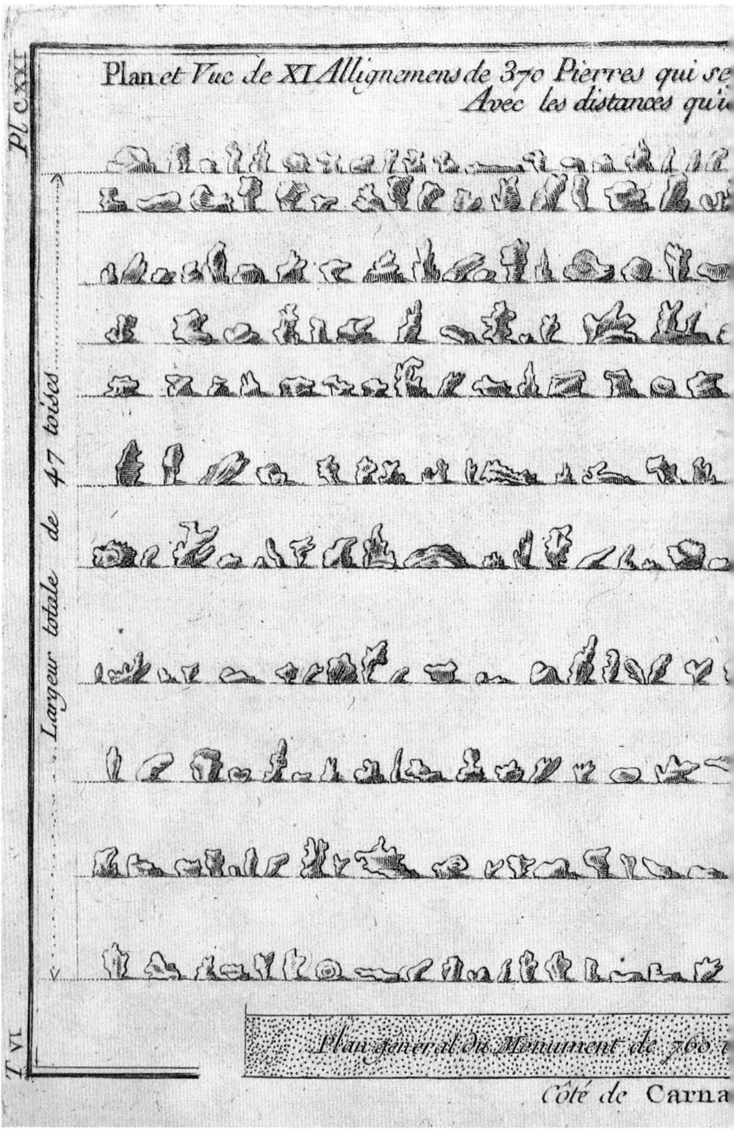

axis between the observer and the point where the sun rises on the horizon at the summer solstice. This work was undertaken with the British astronomer Sir Norman Lockyer between 1906 and 1909. The first signs of the science of measurement – metrology – applied to megaliths appeared in 1904 with R. Kerviler's research.

By the end of the 19th century, the first inventories of the megaliths, drawn up in particular by Gabriel and Adrien de Mortillet, were followed by several series of photographs, printed as postcards: more than 1200 cards of Breton megaliths were published between 1900 and 1926! These provide objective information on the way the stones were incorporated into the rural landscape at that time.

Megalithomania and Celtomania

William Stukeley, 1726.

Meanwhile other more intrepid minds were eagerly trying to explain the meaning of the standing stones. In *Megalithomania*, published in 1982, John Michell defines this term as explaining the "monstrous" size of the stones by weird, even oneiric, hypotheses. Most refer to the Celts, long considered responsible for the megaliths, and in particular for the Kermario and Le Ménec alignments. In his book about the celtic world, Jacques de Cambry, the first President of a Celtic academy active between 1804 and 1813, presented the megaliths as Celtic "temples". Drawing inspiration from the romantic poems attributed to the legendary Irish bard Ossian by the poet James Macpherson (1736-1796), he was part of the nationalist tendency of the French Revolution which developed during the First Empire.

Other theories referred to *The Gallic Wars* by Caesar, still our main source of information concerning the Druids in Gaul during the 1st century BC. William Stukeley, an English 18th-century "antiquarian" – or scholar – and his followers were responsible for one of them: Stukeley claimed to reconcile the Christian and Jewish spiritual messages with those of Druidism. He practised "ophiolatry" (from the Greek word *ophis*), or snake worship, identifying its shape in the sinuous lines formed by the menhir alignments, especially at Avebury in England. For him, this cult explained the megalithic religion at which the Druids officiated. A Druidic "Order" was founded in 1781 by Henry Hurle, one of Stukeley's close associates. As early as 1836 Prosper Mérimée, the French general inspector of ancient monuments, took a strong stand against the members of the snake sect. In *Par les champs et les grèves [Over fields and shores]*, published in 1847, Gustave Flaubert held all these lucubrations up to ridicule: "… if I were to be asked, after so many opinions, what is mine, I would give one, irrefutable, undeniable, irresistible … It is as follows: the stones at Carnac are large stones!".

The Druids who gather nowadays in France and England, in particular at Stonehenge, to hold ceremonies honouring the sun on the day of the summer solstice are the heirs to these movements.

Right-hand page and following double page
Druids
Print from *La Création de l'homme, op. cit.*, and photograph of the Druid of Ménez-Hom (Brittany) by Le Doaré, circa 1912.

Pioneers of archaeology

The Kermario menhirs

From October 1877 to April 1878 James Miln, a Scottish traveller enamoured of archaeology, conducted excavations in the Kermario alignments. A precursor of modern archaeology, he noted the exact position of the remains he unearthed and recorded all his observations in writing; they were published in 1881. His attention was caught by Gallo-Roman potsherds which according to him supported the hypothesis of the "Roman camp" formulated by certain antiquarians. However he clearly distinguished the Roman level from that of the much earlier menhir packing stones. The menhirs themselves are described in detail, one after another. The thickness of the layer of topsoil surrounding the packing varied; it contained large quantities of charcoal, fragments of querns, mullers, hammerstones, axes and other polished stones, as well as potsherds designated as Celtic and flints (blades, scrapers and arrowheads).

The Lann-Mané dolmen♦, Kermario

In the megalithic chamber tomb situated at the south-western end of the Kermario alignments, Miln found "Celtic" brown potsherds and a polished diorite axe, blackened by burning. In particular, he discovered a globular polished stone – also diorite – a quartz hammerstone, schist tools, flints, a sandstone whetstone, a diorite grinder and a fine-grained granite polisher. He was the first person to draw the conclusion that the menhirs belonged to the same culture as the dolmens: "It is important", he wrote,

The Saint-Michel tumulus at Carnac. The magnitude of the investigations carried out by Le Rouzic is evident in this watercolour by Saint-Just and Péquart. The meticulous notes and drawings of the funerary cists and grave goods found in them, such as these polished stone axes, bear witness to the high quality of the work carried out by these pioneers (Vannes, Musée d'Archéologie du Morbihan).

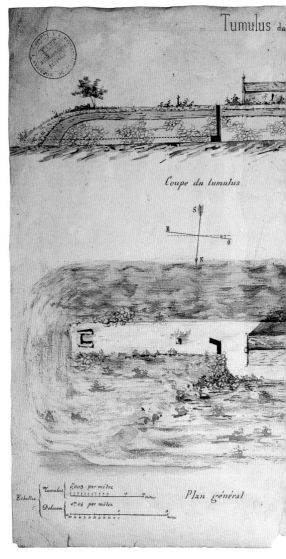

Tumulus du

Coupe du tumulus

Plan général

Echelles { Tumulus 0,003 par mètre
Dolmen 0,04 par mètre

♦ **Tumulus (or barrow):** A mound covering one or several burials, conferring an imposing aspect on cist or chamber tombs; when the mound is composed of small stones, it is called a cairn. The name "Carnac" probably derives from the great cairn of Saint-Michel, situated 400 metres to the north of the church.

"to note here that the objects included in this list are similar to those we have just found under the mound wall and under the menhirs".

The tumulus and giant menhir, Le Manio

Zacharie Le Rouzic – a young man trained by James Miln – and a couple from Nancy who had moved to Carnac, Saint-Just and Marthe Péquart, carried out excavations in 1922 and 1926 in the tumulus♦ of Le Manio 2. They demonstrated its anteriority to the Kermario alignments which, moreover, cover it. Funerary offerings were deposited in two stone cists at the base of a giant menhir during its erection.

Michel en Carnac.

Plan
du dolmen

Coupe suivant AB

Coupe suivant CD

R. Pocard-Keriler du Cozker
d'après Mr R. Galles.

They consisted of vases decorated in the Castellic style, flint arrowheads and querns for grinding grain; most of these offerings were broken and burnt.

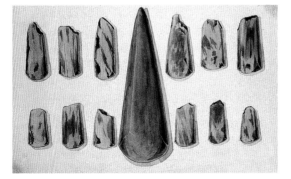

The first restorations

Le Rouzic continued, with greater attention to detail, the work begun by Félix Gaillard, another keen amateur archaeologist, who was in the forefront of activity from 1883 to 1887 He established a dossier for each intervention and placed a red marker on the base of the menhirs which were re-erected. Le Rouzic was appointed a titular member of the French commission for prehistoric monuments in 1933, and continued to devote his time to the restoration of the megaliths until his death in 1939.

A return to the original array of the alignments by re-erecting the fallen menhirs was the aim of early restoration work. Around 1900, numerous postcards presented the gigantic human endeavour in idealised landscapes, either sunny or snow-covered. Drawing (Paris, Bibliothèque des Arts Décoratifs).

Creation of the museum and the guidebook

When James Miln died he left a collection of archaeological objects found during his excavations and stored in two rooms at the *Hôtel des Voyageurs*, Carnac, where he had lived. Premises were built in Carnac to house these precious pieces and inaugurated in 1882. That same year the first version of Félix Gaillard's *Guide et itinéraire illustré [Illustrated guidebook and itinerary]* was published.

A monument of national interest

In 1830 the French State began to set in place a veritable policy for preserving the cultural heritage. In 1837 Mérimée was given the task of drawing up an inventory of monuments worthy of protection. In 1840

Carnac was scheduled as an ancient monument. In 1879 the Minister of Public Instruction and the Fine Arts created a sub-commission for megalithic monuments and appointed Henri Martin as its President. Three months later an inventory of these monuments was published for all of France. A programme of State acquisitions was defined and prosecuted from 1881 to 1889. Félix Gaillard was given the task of negotiating each dossier and in particular, in 1882 and 1883, that of the Le Ménec and Kermario alignments at Carnac. With the help of Louis Cappé, a native of Carnac and Miln's foreman, he had the alignments and dolmens restored and wrote two works: *L'Inventaire des monuments mégalithiques du Morbihan dans le périmètre des acquisitions de l'État [Inventory of megalithic monuments in the Morbihan in the perimeter of the State acquisitions]* (1892) and *L'Astronomie préhistorique [Prehistoric astronomy]* (1895).

The increasing number of visitors to the site threatened the plant cover and the stability of the standing stones; this, together with a growing awareness of the exceptional cultural interest of these alignments, led the State to take action. In 1990, in collaboration with the local authorities, a new development project was decided which combines safeguarding the stones, providing educational information and regulating access to the Kermario, Kerlescan and Le Ménec sites.

Mérimée (1803-1870) was one of the first to understand the "architectural" interest of the alignments. When he went to ascertain their originality for himself, he painted this gouache (private collection).

Child astride a menhir at Kermario. Coloured photograph (Paris, Bibliothèque des Arts Décoratifs).

Around 1900 the alignments of Carnac, Le Ménec, Kermario and Kerlescan were scheduled as ancient monuments and restored. A wide variety of postcards were published for the tourists who were beginning to flock there.

These photographs bear valuable testimony to the state of the stones. The landscape, clear of trees and quite different from that seen today, is probably fairly close to that of the Neolithic period, with its flourishing agricultural way of life.

| **Neolithic house.**
Reconstruction of one of the four buildings whose remains were found on the site of La Hersonnais-en-Pléchâtel (Ille-et-Vilaine).

Megaliths and the Neolithic period

Polished stone axes (jadeite, dolerite and, later, flint). Votive or transformed into pendants, they could form hoards, like that of Arzon in the Morbihan (below: Saint-Germain-en-Laye, Musée des Antiquités Nationales) or be deposited as offerings in chamber tombs (bottom, Vannes, Musée d'Archéologie du Morbihan).

Right-hand page
Axes pecked on one of the slabs at Gavrinis.

Some 18 000 years ago, after the last extremely cold periods of the Upper Palaeolithic, of which traces remain in the cave of Lascaux (Dordogne), the climate grew milder, the ice melted and the sea level rose. In the bay of Quiberon, in 4000 BC, it was still 5 or 6 metres lower than it is now: the Gulf of Morbihan was not under water, Gavrinis was a hill and not an island. The land around Carnac was cultivated or used for grazing; most of the trees were cut down.

First farmers: from the Near East to Brittany

The "Neolithic" way of life, essentially rural, is defined by the domestication of plants and animals, which appeared in the Near East around 8000 BC, together with the establishment of sedentary groups in villages. In the west of France the new production economy is characterised by wheat, barley and sheep, foreign to the regional biotope, or biological environment (they come from the Near East).

Two traditions met and mingled in Brittany: cultures from the Mediterranean region which progressed along the coasts, reaching the Atlantic through the Strait of Gibraltar, and the European "Danubian" culture which originated on the shores

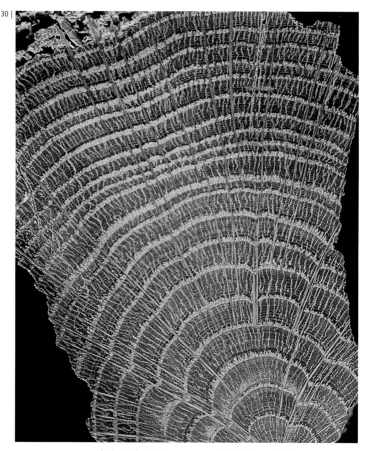

The search for ancient trees from California to the Alps has, thanks to the combination of tree-ring sequences, allowed an absolute chronological scale to be obtained. It goes back at least 10000 years and calibrates the series of dates determined by the radiocarbon (C14) method by adjusting them slightly, since radioactivity levels have not always been completely regular.

of the Black Sea around 6000 BC. This encounter may perhaps be one of the keys to the original features found in the Armorican region: between the 6th and 5th millennia BC, in the area corresponding to modern Poitou, Brittany and Normandy, different practices and social rites seem to have appeared, in particular an ancestor cult which could have legitimised the appropriation of land and its hereditary transmission. The megaliths, a form of religious architecture, would have been its outward, visible symbol. They are specific to these western cultures of the Atlantic zone between 5000 and 2500 BC. The alignments at Carnac, Erdeven, Quiberon and Locmariaquer, among the most spectacular, were erected around 4000 BC.

Dating methods

Since the 1950s the development by laboratories of absolute dating methods, such as those based on Carbon 14, has been spectacular. They have allowed the main periods of prehistory, and the different phases of the Neolithic – when the megalithic alignments were constructed – to be dated. Cross-checking the various methods provides the chronological scale used by scientists. The monuments at Carnac, in particular, have been dated by the radiocarbon method, thanks to the charcoal found among the grave goods. These data have been confirmed by dendrochronology, a method applied to trees from Alpine lake dwellings, contemporary with the alignments. They have been corroborated by potsherds also found in the tombs, dated by thermoluminescence. It can thus now be stated with certainty that the alignments date not from 2000 BC, as was previously believed, but from 4000 BC.

Radiocarbon dating consists of measuring the concentration in radioactive elements of the Carbon 14 (C14) isotope which, absorbed by plants (charcoal) or animals (bones and shells), disintegrates and decays by half every 5 730 years (a duration corresponding to the half-life of the radioactivity of C14). The C14 dosage of the sample thus allows the time having elapsed between the analysis and the death of the organism to be calculated.

Dendrochronology is the study of the annual growth rings of ancient wood, whose patterns vary from year to year. Dendrochronological sequences have been established going as far back as the early Neolithic period. They allow C14 dates to be refined and sometimes "corrected" for periods when radioactivity was not quite regular.

A third method, thermoluminescence, is increasingly used for the Neolithic period: it dates the luminescence emitted by the crystals of a rock or piece of pottery when they are heated (cooking, fire, volcanic eruption); this emission of light is proportional to the duration separating their reheating in the laboratory from the last time they were heated during prehistoric times.

The radiocarbon (C14) method allows the dating of any sample of organic material: wood or charcoal, bone, shell, leather, plant or animal fibres.

Who built the megaliths?

Above and right-hand page
Tombs at Téviec (Morbihan).
Viewed during the excavations and reconstructed in the museum at Carnac; they herald megalithic tombs.

Green variscite necklaces.
Grave goods deposited in chamber tombs or cists (top, Vannes, Musée d'Archéologie; bottom, Saint-Germain-en-Laye, Musée des Antiquités Nationales).

Data concerning the morphology of the Neolithic inhabitants of the region of Carnac are scarce as the Breton soil is often acid and dissolves bone. It is however possible to have a fairly precise idea of the population. Human skeletons found a few kilometres from Carnac in the islands of Téviec and Hoëdic (Morbihan), which were then attached to the continent, constitute a reference series. They belong to members of a group of hunters who lived around 6000 BC. They domesticated animals (dogs and perhaps sheep) and practised the collective burial of their dead, two features indicating a way of life close to the Neolithic. Eleven men, twelve women and thirteen children or newborn infants have been identified. They were gracile (i.e. of slender build) and not very tall: 1.59 metres on average for the men and 1.51 for the women. Their hands are sturdy, their feet small and their narrow skull broadens at the face. A few remains have been found in megalithic tombs: that of La Torche-en-Ploemeur (Finistère) held five to ten bodies and archaeological artefacts dating from the Middle Neolithic (around 4000 BC); in the Quiberon Peninsula, seven skeletons have been found at Conguel and some forty individuals at Port-Blanc. They date from the Late Neolithic (4th millennium BC).

The builders of the megaliths found along the Atlantic coast were no different from the other Neolithic populations of Europe. Megalithic prowess is not due to any special physical strength but to an excellent organisation of work. Erecting such stones required a hierarchical society: a leader – i.e. a single will and much diplomacy to convince the population – architects who knew about the resistance of materials and could master measurements, priests who federated the faith of the inhabitants, and manpower.

Where did they live?

The hundred or so megalithic monuments recorded in the Carnac region seem to point to a large population. The construction of megaliths (the heaviest weighs 300 tonnes) must have mobilised several hundred men, which implies a population of several thousand inhabitants.

At Croh-Collé on the Quiberon Peninsula coast, humble hut circles have been found in a village defended by a ditch and a fairly low rampart. The numerous hearths disposed on paved areas of the Er-Yoh islet near the island of Houat (Morbihan) were sheltered in the hollows of rocks and marked off by low walls. People ate a fairly varied selection of meat: bones found include those of sheep and small cattle, some large cattle, pigs and wild boars. Occasionally Neolithic man hunted hares, rabbits, beavers and seals, and more rarely deer and small horses. They also ate sea birds – guillemots and razorbills, gulls and cormorants – fished, mainly labridae like wrasse, and collected seafood such as patellae, mussels and clams. Several querns and grinders prove that they also ground cereals into flour which they cooked as a sort of pancake and as gruel. These numerous traces of scattered, probably seasonal, dwellings cannot be assimilated to an organised and structured village. The site of Curnic-en-Guissény (Finistère), on the other hand, is more like one, with its hearths, millstones, pottery, polished stone axes, flint knapping working areas, etc.

Research regarding dwelling remains should provide information on the territorial organisation around the Gulf of Morbihan. It is unfortunately more than likely that the sea, whose level has risen by 5 to 6 metres since Neolithic times, has destroyed most of the sites established on the foreshore.

Below
Millstone and grinder, pottery vases, evoke everyday life whereas prestigious objects suggest communications, trade and diplomacy; Breton chamber tombs (Saint-Germain-en-Laye, Musée des Antiquités Nationales).

Following double page **Offerings** from the Le Manio tumulus (Carnac, Musée de Préhistoire).

Megaliths in Western Europe

The "megalithic phenomenon" appeared in Portugal, the west of France and probably on the shores of the North Sea during the first half of the 5th millennium BC. It ended between 2000 and 1500 BC, at the beginning of the Bronze Age.

Megaliths were employed in two principal domains which developed concurrently. The first corresponds to an open style of architecture with standing stones or menhirs, either isolated or grouped in alignments and enclosures♦, designating a sacred place. Examples include the giant menhirs measuring between 6 and 20 metres (the record reached by the decorated menhir of Locmariaquer, circa 4300 BC), the Carnac alignments (circa 4000 BC) and Stonehenge (between 3000 and 1500 BC), with its characteristic trilithons. The second is a closed style of architecture with cists and chamber tombs, sometimes accessible by passages and covered by mounds.

Megalithic chamber tombs are related to an ancestor cult. A comparative study of their architecture allows the history of megalithic building to be

♦Enclosure:
*Any closed form
constructed with
standing stones,
joined edge-
to-edge or merely
placed close
together.
A standing stone
enclosure may be
circular, oval
or rectangular.*

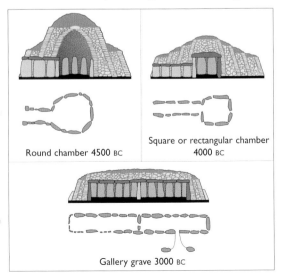

The three main types of megalithic passage tombs: circular chamber roofed with dry-stone corbelling; rectangular chamber covered with a capstone; elongated chamber with a lateral entrance and roofed with slabs placed alongside one another.

Round chamber 4500 BC

Square or rectangular chamber 4000 BC

Gallery grave 3000 BC

38 | Table des Marchands, Locmariaquer (Morbihan). "Dolmen" first designated a stone table. Print from *Essai sur des monuments armoricains* […], op. cit.

The remains of the walls or facings of the protective tumulus appear during the excavations carried out between 1986 and 1994 by J. L'Helgouach, S. Cassen and C.-T. Le Roux.

The structured tumulus (called "cairn" in Breton) surrounding this passage tomb, reconstructed as it was conceived in Neolithic times, with the Locmariaquer Grand Menhir brisé in the background.

followed between 4500 and 1500 BC. The earliest forms could be pits containing cists, later found in huge long barrows such as the Saint-Michel tumulus at Carnac (circa 4500 BC). At the same time, some tombs have a round chamber with a corbelled vault reached by a passage whose walls consist of large stones. They are also found under great mounds, for example at Barnenez (Plouezoch, Finistère) and in two of the cairns at Bougon (Deux-Sèvres). Around 4000 BC tombs with trapezoidal or quadrangular chambers and a passage appear in round barrows: the best examples include the "Table des Marchands" at Locmariaquer (Morbihan),

Gavrinis at Larmor-Baden (Morbihan), and some of the tombs in the cairns at Bougon (Deux-Sèvres). Around 3500 BC in Ireland (Newgrange and Knowth), the burial chamber in some passage tombs♦ may be divided or have subsidiary cells forming a sort of transept. Others, like the monument called "Les Pierres Plates" at Locmariaquer (Morbihan), have an elongated quadrangular chamber, which may be either straight or angled, and a short passage. Around 3000 BC gallery graves♦ also present elongated quadrangular chambers and an antechamber. Cists, built with reused stones, were installed in round mounds until around 1500 BC.

The Neolithic inhabitants of the Atlantic coast impressed all their successors by the megalithic monuments they erected. These landmarks prove that "land domestication" was an acquired fact. However, they also play a role linked to the sky: their orientation, their position calculated in relationship to the course of the sun – and perhaps of the moon – imply a certain degree of knowledge in the field of astronomy which was no less remarkable for being empirical.

♦**Passage tomb:** *A type of chamber tomb characterised by a mound covering a burial chamber approached by a narrow entrance passage.*

♦**Gallery grave:** *A form of elongated chamber tomb in which there is no distinction between the entrance passage and the burial chamber proper (also known by its French name, allée couverte).*

Table des Marchands, interior view with its crook-decorated headstone and its capstone. The latter, like that of the tomb at Gavrinis, comes from an earlier giant menhir.

Megalithic art: symbolic images

One of the characteristics of megaliths in Western Europe is the fact that they are decorated with more or less recognisable motifs executed by picking or pecking the stone. Some pictograms are found in the Breton system, dating from the 5th to the 4th millennium: they represent arms and tools – a bow and its arrows (Gavrinis), axes, hafted or not (Barnenez, Gavrinis), a stylised sperm whale (Grand Menhir Brisé, Gavrinis) or yet again a crosier or shepherd's crook (Guennoc, Table des Marchands). The animal kingdom is not forgotten: a horn-like shape could be a rough representation of a bull at Gavrinis and Locmariaquer, a snake (a sinuous line with or without a head) has been identified at Le Manio and Gavrinis. An emblematic figure, the "buckler idol", ogival with lateral recesses and appendages,

Stylised idols: Examples from the dolmens of Les Pierres Plates, Mané Er Hroek at Locmariaquer and Luffang (Morbihan) show how varied these emblematic images could be.

Snakes, axes, crooks and idols (buckler motif), slab in the passage at Gavrinis (Morbihan).

The main motifs found in megalithic art in the Morbihan, top to bottom: idol (buckler), stylised sperm whale, crook, axe, bovine horns, ox or bull, snakes.

sometimes with "hairs" radiating from the upper section, is found at an early date at Barnenez and sometimes adopts monumental proportions: for example the large idol of Petit-Mont and the one which serves as the back stone for the Table des Marchands.

Some statues in the form of idols, later in date (around 3000 BC) have breasts. Some slabs, merely decorated with carved breasts, sometimes accompanied by a necklace, seem to confirm the feminine nature of this higher being, the "mother-goddess". When present, she dominates all the emblems of masculine power: bow, axe, crook, but also bulls and snakes. In the Neolithic religion connected with the megaliths of western Europe, men seem rarely to be represented, unlike women. This is true also for other regions: the many statuettes from Neolithic central Europe are almost exclusively feminine, exactly like the iconography found in the Mediterranean region at the same period, whether in the west (Sardinia and Malta) or east (as far as Çatal Hüyük in Anatolia).

Another centre of megalithic art exists in Portugal, where motifs include snakes, goblets, hunters' arms, geometrical figures and probably the sun and the moon. The use of red paint is noteworthy. The Irish centre of megalithic art – all spirals, stars, dots and zigzags – is later (4th millennium) and more abstract.

Stones circles and giant menhirs

Over the past twenty years various discoveries have rekindled the interest of researchers, whose curiosity had already been aroused by certain British ceremonial sites.

Avebury (Wiltshire), not far from Stonehenge, is a gigantic ditch (400 metres in diameter) with a circle of standing stones around its inner lip and two smaller circles in the central area. Two rows of standing stones lead from one of the four entrances to another structure situated about 2.5 km to the south. Stonehenge (Wiltshire) is a circle of standing stones,

Almendres
(Portugal),
circle of standing
stones, some
decorated with
simple motifs
such as circles
or crooks.
This is one
of the earliest
circles in Europe,
dating from the
5th millennium BC.

used for one thousand five hundred years between 3000 and 1500 BC. The horseshoe-shaped centre is completed by an alignment called "the Avenue" leading to the Heel Stone, i.e. the stone which, for an observer placed in the centre of the monument, indicates the point where the sun appears in the east on the day of the summer solstice.

Callanish (Lewis) has a circle of standing stones on a mound covering an earlier central chamber tomb, from which three rows of menhirs lead east, south and west, while a double row extends 70 to 80 metres towards the north.

The triple alignment of standing stones at Mid Clyth, Caithness (Highland Region) is arranged in a fan shape along a median north-south axis. Archaeologists have sometimes compared this site with that of Kerlescan at Carnac.

Maes Howe in the Orkneys (Scotland) and the huge circle at **Avebury** in Wiltshire (England), two famous sites for standing stones.

The tapering standing stones in the Orkneys are perfectly integrated in the landscape and are found close to megalithic funerary monuments.

Among the sixty or so alignments known in Brittany, the 19 giant menhirs of Locmariaquer (Morbihan) form an impressive rectilinear system. They were erected in the late 5th millennium BC then destroyed by later Neolithic inhabitants who reused them to build dolmens.

The aligned menhirs of Cojoux at Saint-Just (Ille-et-Vilaine) first consisted of quartz blocks placed between hearths dating from the mid-5th millennium. In a second phase, large slabs and wooden posts were arranged along the same axis, then funerary deposits were made alongside certain recumbent monoliths.

The site of Monteneuf (Morbihan) is an incomplete menhir system, orientated east-west, which could be compared with that of Carnac. There is some evidence pointing to a presence on the site by the end of the 5th millennium, but the construction seems later and in use around 3300 BC.

The series of alignments at Yverdon and Lutry (Switzerland), dating from between 3800 and

The standing stone system at Callanish (Lewis, Outer Hebrides) indicates the points of the compass from a circle.

Grand Menhir Brisé, Locmariaquer. This huge monolith, the largest in Western European prehistory, measures 20 metres and weighs 300 tonnes. It was erected (drawing on the left) before being brought down and broken into four pieces.

3000 BC, seem to be commemorative stelae with anthropomorphic profiles. They are orientated approximately east-west. The transition from simple menhir to anthropomorphic menhir appears in Corsica. The circle of menhirs – at first single then later double – at Almendres near Evora (Portugal) was apparently frequented from the 5th to the 3rd millennium BC. Some stones are decorated with crooks, snakes and, at the end of the Neolithic period, faces.

Characteristics of the Carnac alignments

The Kerlescan alignments. Cleuziou's plan shows the complementarity between the rows of menhirs and the western enclosure.

Among the seven alignments of the Carnac region the Kerlescan lines, including 579 menhirs, present a very legible configuration. The thirteen rows of stones are arranged in a fan shape over a length of 350 metres. They lead, on the west, to a quadrangular enclosure 80 metres wide by 90 metres long, demarcated on three sides by standing stones 2 to 2.5 metres tall and, on the north side, by a long barrow with a terminal menhir. Other remains have been recorded near Kerlescan. A large menhir, called the Le Manio "Giant", stands 400 metres to the west. A vast hemicycle of menhirs and a megalithic tomb with a side entrance in a long barrow is situated to the north. The alignments of Le Petit-Ménec begin 400 metres to the east.

To the south-west of Kerlescan, the Kermario system, with a general north-east/south-west orientation, is the largest; it extends over 1100 metres and includes 982 menhirs. The alignments consist of ten approximately parallel rows of menhirs, about 100 metres apart and laid out in a hollow. The terrain rises to the edge of a high point situated to the west: it is there that the stones are the tallest, an arrangement similar to those of Kerlescan and Le Ménec. In the western section of Kermario an enclosure constructed of standing stones probably existed, as indicated by the pile of menhirs mentioned on a plan drawn in 1881 by James Miln.

To the south-west of Kermario, the Le Ménec alignments still include 1169 menhirs laid out over 950 metres. The eleven rows of standing stones, here too with a general north-east/south-west orientation, present the same characteristics as the other two systems. At the western end, the remains of an oval enclosure measuring 90 metres by 70 metres, marked out by menhirs set edge-to-edge, are still visible: 71 stones surround the modern houses. The Le Ménec "Giant", 3.5 metres tall, stands out by its tapered shape. It is set off to the north in relationship to the rows of menhirs and is probably earlier than the alignments.

After legends and folklore, early attempts to find explanations, the first surveys and excavations and then the contribution of scientific dating methods, a new phase is heralded: a general research project is essential to verify that each stone is indeed in its original place and better identify all indications concerning the prehistoric frequentation of the site. A new inventory has just been completed; the number of menhirs in place is around 2730. Finally, more widespread surveys are bringing to light other monuments whose relationship with the alignments had never previously been recognised.

The best known alignments at Carnac, those of **Le Ménec, Kermario** and **Kerlescan,** have to be compared with other similar systems, less well-preserved but just as characteristic, for example Kerzerho at Erdeven, Sainte-Barbe and Le Moulin at Plouharnel (from top to bottom).

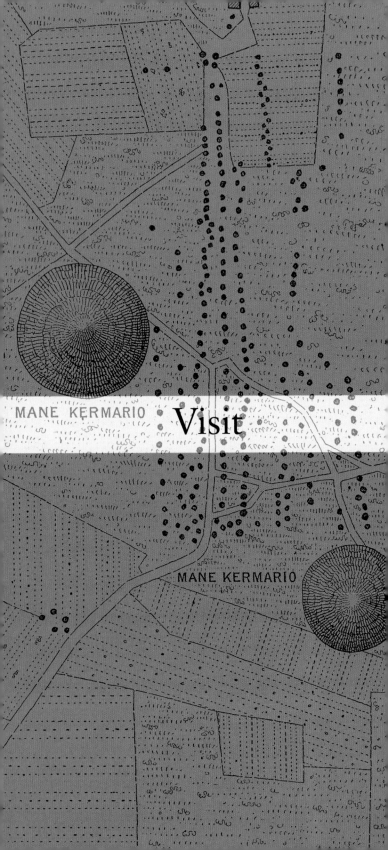

MANE KERMARIO · Visit

MANE KERMARIO

The Carnac alignments

*The site of Kermario may be chosen as an introduction
to the megalithic sites of the region of Carnac
for several reasons: it is situated in the centre of the other
alignments; it is close to the village of Carnac,
its museum and the Saint-Michel tumulus.
However, visitors interested in alignments can opt
for starting with the discovery
of the alignments at Kerlescan or Ménec.*

House of Megalithes— Information Center

Information on the background of research concerning the Carnac alignments is freely available to the public. A model allows visitors to locate their position and appreciate the magnitude of the alignments. A projection room and bookshop complete the services of the centre.

Eight stages of discovery

To understand what an alignment is means taking an interest in the standing stones, how they were set in place, their state of conservation, the units of measurement and geometry of the architecture, the topography and landscape, orientations, construction phases and chronology – not forgetting the hypothesis of a Neolithic temple.

Model of the Kermario alignments.

Stage 1:
The Carnac granite standing stones

The menhirs of the Carnac alignments are stones which are not found in their natural position. They have been manipulated in order to be seen. Generally oblong or slab-shaped, they have been fixed in the ground and stand vertically pointing towards the sky. The erect stone thus presents a visible section and one hidden in the ground, wedged in a shallow dug-out hollow filled with small packing stones.

The menhirs in the alignments are fine-grained Carnac granite. This rock comes from the massif where the stones have been installed, part of the Cornish anticlinal zone♦. The stones were thus procured locally.

On closer observation, three facies of this granite can be distinguished, which will perhaps allow the identification of series of menhirs which come from exactly the same area: a facies with fine grains from 1 to 3 mm, with feldspar and two micas, rich in biotite and poor in micas; a pseudoporphyritic facies, with fairly large quartz and feldspar crystals often exceeding 1 cm and reaching 4 cm, a majority of biotite associated with zircon and very little muscovite; an intermediate granular facies with coarse grains of 1 to 5 mm including feldspar crystals and sporadic concentrations of biotite. This last facies seems the most widespread both on the ground and as far as the menhirs are concerned. All the grains are consolidated in a compact texture but, in certain eroded zones, they form a horizontal lamellar layer in the rocky mass. When the menhirs are standing, this layer is vertical, proof of the human action which erected them.

The weight of the menhirs is estimated by multiplying their approximate volume (height by width by thickness) by the density of granite, i.e. 2.4.

Seen under the microscope, the grains of the granite are clearly visible, in particular the micas.

♦ **Cornish anticlinal zone:** A huge geological convex fold, affecting the south of England (Cornwall) and Brittany.

Stage 2: Strange forms

The menhirs, set one behind another, have more or less regular shapes but some stand out by their truly strange forms: a small foot and big head, a large belly and arched back, a wide groove around the edge, etc. These details are interesting, for they provide information on the geological background and origin of the blocks when they were in place in the rock mass. This presents surface cracks, which opened when the granitic mass cooled during the geological formation of the primary strata (the geological substratum of the primary era, set in place more than 225 million years ago).

The strange forms of the menhirs can be explained by the very ancient erosion of their original rock substratum.

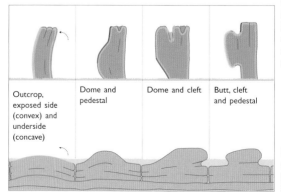

| Outcrop, exposed side (convex) and underside (concave) | Dome and pedestal | Dome and cleft | Butt, cleft and pedestal |

Extracting menhirs (after Dominique Sellier).

Ceorges Des

Setting in place a standing stone using wooden levers, ropes and abundant manpower. Print from *La Création de l'homme [...]*, op. cit.

The vertical cracks, often widened through erosion, are perpendicular to one another. They naturally form slabs, one or several metres long and one to two metres wide, when a horizontal crack has occurred along a lamellar grain layer, at a depth of 0.50 to 1 metre. Thus, natural menhirs could have been found on the moor. In other cases, the stone was affected by vertical cracks, but had to be extracted from the rock base using hammerstones, wooden wedges and levers to help cleave the rock along a fragile stratum of grains.

Extraction

To remove yet other monoliths the rock itself had to be

attacked: striking with hammerstones caused vertical cracks which had to be widened to produce the horizontal cleavage crack required to remove the block. The menhirs thus present either reliefs resulting from pre-megalithic geological erosion or cutting marks due to the alignments' builders. Fresh wear marks corresponding to the erosion of the stone since its erection can generally be perceived. Surveys should enable the menhirs' quarry sites, probably close to the alignments, to be identified.

Transport

On somes sites, a relatively important distance separates

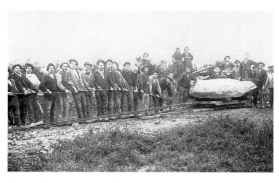

Hauling a slab from the Kerhan dolmen at Saint-Philibert (Morbihan) organised by Le Rouzic in 1896 to transport the dolmen to Meudon (Hauts-de-Seine).

the menhir from its original rock. This means the menhir was brought from further afield and transported to its final location. The granite menhir of Champ-Dolent, near Dol, is on a plateau with a schistose substratum; the 125-tonne block was dragged over four kilometres. The Derlez-en-Peumérit (Finistère) menhir was moved three kilometres. One of the slabs in a cairn at Bougon (Deux-Sèvres), weighing 32 tonnes, came from a limestone quarry (flint-bearing Bathonian) situated four kilometres from the site. An experiment in 1979 demonstrated that the block could be dragged 100 metres in one day by 200 people. About forty days were therefore required to take it to the necropolis. The transport of average-weight blocks (between five and ten tonnes) was easily carried out with wooden rollers and ropes.

Setting in place

The bases of the menhirs were set in pits, meticulously prepared with packing stones, for example in the Kermario alignments – as James Miln proved during his excavations in the late 19th century – and at Locmariaquer, at the base of the Grand Menhir Brisé (now fallen), and in the nineteen other hollows intended for other giant menhirs.

The difficulty must certainly have been to manage to have the end of the stone pivot by raising it so that it slid slowly into its socket. A gin♦ was probably used. Some ingenious minds have even imagined

a wooden box filled with sand which, as it poured out, would have ensured a slower descent of the stone into its pit and thus helped to avoid breaking it. To succeed in this delicate operation a ramp or a crib – a scaffolding of crossed timbers – was perhaps necessary.

Foundation ceremony

Excavations at the base of the menhirs (partial if they are standing, to avoid destabilising them, total if they have fallen) have established that before the stone was set in place there was a ritual deposit and thus a foundation ceremony. The evidence includes charcoal and stones reddened by a high temperature, together with potsherds, flint flakes and tools, polished stone axes, querns or grinders, polishers and spindle-whorls♦. Miln found such remains in large quantities at the base of the Kermario menhirs during his excavations, published in 1881.

♦**Gin:**
A mechanical apparatus used for hoisting heavy weights, usually a tripod with a pulley.

♦**Spindle-whorl:**
A disc-shaped object with a central perforation, made of stone or baked clay, used to weight the thread the spinner forms by twisting the raw fibres held on the spindle.

Erection of an experimental menhir in 1997 at Bougon (Deux-Sèvres) by the members of a Vendean megalithic study group. In the foreground, the pit and the packing stones.

Stage 3: Intact and deteriorated stones

Careful observation of the menhirs therefore provides information on their setting in place and history based on their eroded forms and more or less strange shapes. These very worn pre-megalithic reliefs, which can be explained by a horizontal rather than vertical position of the stone, differ from removals and impacts contemporary with its setting in place, and from erosion reliefs due to its ageing. Grooves caused by rainwater streaming from hollows formed on the top appear more on the south sides; they are filled with moss and lichen. Basins form when the grooves widen by the combined effect of rainwater (735 mm on average per year) and wind which removes grains from the stone, in particular – in view of the prevailing winds – on the west and south sides.

Natural erosion

Deterioration of this type can prove that the menhirs in question have not been moved since the Neolithic period. Dominique Sellier has verified that in the Kerlescan alignments 50% of the menhirs were intact and standing in their original position. An extensive enquiry carried out by the Brittany cultural affairs department reached similar conclusions.

Damage caused by Man

Other deterioration due to human action may affect the menhirs. Some, for example, bear traces of attempts to cut off the top, and notches on the sides. Traces of flakes and exfoliation, lighter in colour, then appear on the surface of the stones. It is sometimes difficult to know whether they result from natural deterioration or from human intervention. In fact, they are not numerous and it may be presumed that a large percentage of the menhirs still present the same morphology, and therefore the same aspect, as in Neolithic times. Their surface is often covered with superposed layers of lichen, probably recent. The stone itself may be healthy and compact. It may also present a superficial granular deterioration which makes it rough to the touch, or be affected to a greater degree, when polygonal networks form.

A relatively good condition?

This relatively good state of conservation of the menhirs' surface means it is possible to search for Neolithic engraved or picked motifs, such as the snakes at the base of the Le Manio "Giant" near the eastern section of the Kermario alignments, the hafted axe on the Grand Menhir Brisé at Locmariaquer, or the crooks on the Kermarquer menhir at Moustoirac.

These grooves formed by rainwater retained in a hollow on the top of the stone are due to erosion. Moss and lichen grow there in abundance. On some stones, large areas have remained intact since Neolithic times and careful examination reveals pecked and perhaps engraved motifs (Grand Menhir Brisé, Locmariaquer).

Stage 4:
Units of
measurement
and geometry

Several systematic surveys of
the Carnac alignments have been
carried out, in particular by
the Scotsman Miln, the German
Schuchardt and the Austrian
Mondrijan. It was however
between 1970 and 1976 that a
former professor of engineering
science at Oxford, the Scotsman
Alexander Thom, confirmed,
on a statistical basis, the use
by the builders of megaliths of
a standard unit of length. With
the help of British and American
foundations and many specialists,
including his son A. S. Thom and
R. L. Merritt, he worked
on the diameters of British
circles and the spaces between
Breton menhirs.

This average unit of length, called
the megalithic yard, is equal
to 0.829 metres and corresponds
to the "pace" defined a century
ago by the mathematician

R. Kerviler. The other unit,
more specific to Carnac,
called the megalithic *toise,*
or fathom, is equivalent
to 2.5 yards or 2.073 metres.
The only possible assessment
of these units is statistical,
for the very volume of
the stones means their centre
has to be taken as the basis
for calculations. The standard
nature of the distances
separating the centre of one
stone from the centre of the
next points to a high degree
of rationalisation in the
construction of these types of
architecture. How did Neolithic

**The Le Ménec
system,**
at the far
western end
of the Carnac
alignments,
includes
a cromlech,
or enclosure of
standing stones.
Slabs belonging to
this enclosure are
still visible (left).
The geometry
of this oval
was perhaps
constructed
with the help
of a right-angled
triangle
(below, after
Thom).

The sun throws shadows which accentuate the regularity of the menhirs' layout. As shown by the graduated scale (left side of the photograph) the whole space is thus measured by a system which is both human and solar.

The menhirs are intended to be seen from afar in a sort of huge garden. When Nature regains possession of the land, ferns and pines submerge the standing stones, which disappear from sight.

man devise these units of measurement, and how were they transmitted? That remains a mystery. In spite of the difference between the megalithic yard and *toise* it remains true that they both derive from a standard system of measurement.

In each of the lines at Le Ménec and Kermario, Alexander Thom and his son demonstrated that the gap between each stone, in every row, was equal to the megalithic *toise*. Nevertheless it remains to be verified that each menhir is indeed in its original position before this unit of measurement can be definitively validated. Thom believes that a simple multiple of it was also used to define the diameter of the circles of standing stones or to build other types of cromlechs♦. This high degree of precision is proved true, even when the alignments "meander" because of the topography, irregularities in the rocky ground in which they stand, or an approximate re-installation of some stones.

♦*Cromlech:* *A Welsh word designating stones arranged in a circle; the walls of a megalithic chamber whose capstone has generally disappeared. By extension, the name cromlech has often been given in Brittany to any circular or quadrangular enclosure.*

Stage 5: Stones in a well-tended landscape

Standing stones are erected to be seen. This observation suggests a close relationship between the menhirs and the moor landscape in which they are inserted. The ecological and spatial characteristics of the Carnac alignments are indispensable factors in understanding the monument and safeguarding the site.

Protection of the plant cover is essential; its deterioration or disappearance because of too many visitors trampling on it seriously threatens the very stability of the menhirs, whose bases become exposed.

The vast scale of the Carnac alignments is related to the moor landscape. Postcards dating from the early 20th century bear witness to the existence of grass. Studies of ancient pollen, made on samples taken from neighbouring marshland, reveal that this situation dates back to the beginning of the Neolithic period, when the forest was cut back to make way for fields and meadows. Climatic change over the past 6 000 years has not been enough for the landscape to have radically changed. However moorland, like pasture, has to be looked after; man, depending on the season, has to mow it or bring in animals (Breton moorland sheep, which are light and do not break up the ground). If it is not looked after, the moor returns to its wooded state. This natural ecosystem prevails at present on the edges of the sites. It is devastating for the alignments: the stones are shaken by the roots of the trees, mainly oaks, dog-roses, acacias, some birch and, more recently, pines. In order to restore their initial plant surroundings to the Carnac megaliths, botanists from the university of Rennes are concentrating their research on the formation of two types of moorland, dry moor with slow growth and more humid moor with faster growth (bracken, broom and heather).

Stage 6: Orientations

The orientations of the Carnac alignments seem to satisfy two types of logic. The first is geographic and follows the edge of the continental plateau of the granitic massif which stands 30 metres above the coastal zone of sediments carried by the rivers flowing into the sea. The second coincides with the main points of the compass, in particular the east-west axis. The various alignments present approximate orientations, but the general system of the stones' layout is nonetheless homogeneous.

According to Professor Alexander Thom, two cromlechs in particular seem to have been built following more precise orientation criteria. The first, that of the Kerlescan alignments, could indicate the two solstices (summer and winter) on each side of the general axis of the alignment, which corresponds to that of the equinox♦. A seasonal calendar of ceremonies related

Bullfinches, heather and broom are part of the menhirs' existence.

♦ **Equinox:** *The date when the position of the sun is such that day and night are of equal length, i.e. about 21 March (spring equinox in the northern hemisphere) and 23 September (autumn equinox).*

The heath around the alignments needs annual mowing and grazing by sheep.

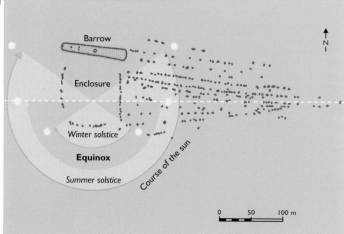

Barrow

Enclosure

Winter solstice

Equinox

Summer solstice

Course of the sun

N

0   50   100 m

The Kerlescan site, with its alignments and its enclosure, presents, for an observer standing in the centre of the enclosure, the prime directions of the rising and setting of the sun.

Vase decorated in the Castellic style (top) and perfume-burner or pedestal cup (side view, middle, and vertical view, bottom).

to rural activities could have been drawn up, based on these landmarks. This same layout is found in the rectangular Crucuno enclosure at Plouharnel. It probably allowed the extreme positions of the rising and setting of the sun to be determined for the winter and summer solstices and the two equinoxes.

The importance of the cromlechs or enclosures installed to the west of the alignments is all the more perceptible in that they occupy a high spot in the landscape. No visitor walking from the east along the rows of menhirs can fail to be impressed by the closed structure of the enclosure composed of large standing stones on the western horizon. Another hypothesis proposed by Alexander Thom cannot however be accepted.

It is that the Carnac alignments belong to a vast observatory, involving the alignments, the Grand Menhir Brisé at Locmariaquer and some large barrows. Excavations carried out by Jean L'Helgouach, Serge Cassen and Charles-Tanguy Le Roux indicated, some ten years ago, that the Grand Menhir belonged in fact to a series of 19 aligned stones, probably set in place well before the menhirs of the alignments. The functional relationship between the two sites is not therefore founded.

Stage 7: Construction phases and chronology

Dating the Carnac alignments calls for archaeological observations and deductions: there are no dates determined directly on samples (charcoal or pottery) taken from the base of the Carnac standing stones.

The giant menhirs

Excavations in the Le Manio barrow (in the Kermario alignments) have shown that, in a first phase, the menhirs were fixed in the mound, following the same direction: they were therefore later than it. The Le Manio "Giant", a six-metre tall menhir with engravings of snakes at its base, dates from the construction of the barrow; it can be compared with the great menhirs of Locmariaquer, associated with pottery of the late 5th millennium BC Castellic style found at the base of the great stones.

Tombs with a rectangular chamber

The following phase corresponds to the construction of tombs with a rectangular chamber, around 4000 BC. At Kermario, a tomb with a passage and a trapezoidal chamber which still has part

of its mound was built inside the area presumed to correspond to the enclosure related to these alignments. If the relationship between this tomb and the alignments really exists the standing stones would have been set in place circa 4000 BC. The homogeneity of the alignments would then indicate that the erection phase for the stones was fairly rapid. Their ceremonial function doubtless lasted a long time, so minor additions and modifications could have taken place over the course of time.

Tombs with long chambers

The long megalithic tomb with a lateral entrance apparently corresponds to a third phase of use of the site. Built around 3000 BC, following the same orientation as the general axis of the Kerlescan

alignment but outside it, it seems to be much later. Its layout reveals the intention of including this tomb in the general ceremonial orientation of the monument.

This confirms that a close relationship lasted several centuries between the sacred and ceremonial function of the alignments and the funerary function of certain tombs.

The Le Manio tumulus (bottom diagram), covered by the menhirs of the eastern section of Kermario, is marked by a **giant menhir** (top) whose base bears picked **snake motifs** (centre).

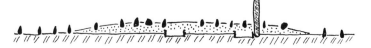

Sunrise at Kermario, from the western area of the enclosure. The Carnac alignments have a cosmic dimension.

Stage 8: Hypothesis of a Neolithic temple

The Neolithic temples at Carnac, with that of Kerlescan in the foreground. The topography is used to locate the place of worship, the enclosures, on higher ground and to the west, and to accentuate the processional function of the alignments (J.-P. Mohen after J.-C. Golvin).

The seven series of alignments in the Carnac region – Le Ménec, Kermario and Kerlescan at Carnac itself, Le Petit-Ménec at La Trinité-sur-Mer, Erdeven, Sainte-Barbe at Plouharnel and Le Moulin at Saint-Pierre-Quiberon – have several features in common: their rows of menhirs are generally parallel; the western end of the alignments, and sometimes their eastern end, terminates in an enclosure; they are characterised by a system of alignments associated with the enclosure, orientated approximately east-west; their topography shows the western enclosure

to advantage on higher ground, while the alignments occupy the eastern slope; finally, all have menhirs whose height increases the closer they are to the enclosure.

The most frequently admitted hypothesis is that the Carnac alignments are places for ceremonies. They are formed of processional alleys bordered by menhirs which lead, on the west, to a place of worship marked by an enclosure situated on a height. The whole system is orientated in such a way that the rays of the rising sun follow the avenues up to the enclosure and, during the evening ceremony, the setting sun bathes the divine place of worship with its last rays. A sacred way and the holy of holies – the enclosure – constitute the elements of the first temple ever built: the Neolithic temple.
In the enclosures at Er Lannic (Morbihan) Zacharie Le Rouzic found hearths, stone cists containing human bones and countless decorated cylindrical vases with bowls – doubtless offering vases or perfume burners – which would confirm the religious nature of the enclosures and, probably, of the alignments associated with them.

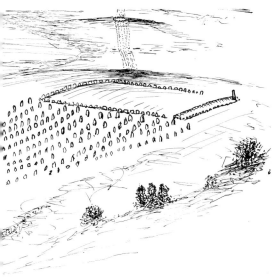

The Kerlescan enclosure, seen from the west in the direction of the equinox. The alignments are visible between two of its stones: the two functions of a temple, processional and ceremonial or ritual, are united.

Other recommended itineraries

The short visit of the Kermario alignments, which includes eight stages of discovery, can be completed by three itineraries recommended to good walkers or cyclists. All three start at the Kermaux mill.

Tour of the Kermario alignments

Follow the eastern section of the Kermario alignments, covering the Le Manio long barrow, easily identified by the great menhir which dominates the landscape. Return by the road and continue along it to skirt the long southern side of the alignments: the menhirs grow taller as they approach the western end.
There visitors will find the Lann-Mané-Kermario dolmen, built on the site of the enclosure which has disappeared but whose location can be identified on the high ground overlooking the alignments.

Visit of the Kerlescan alignments

Follow the path to the west of the Kermario alignments to a wooded and undulating area: on the left the Le Manio Giant and the Le Manio quadrilateral enclosure stand alone.
Slightly further on, the Kerlescan alignments, shorter than those of Kermario and Le Ménec, are particularly distinct with their rows of monoliths converging towards the east and the spectacular quadrilateral enclosure closed on its north side by a long barrow surrounded by small oblique slabs and marked to the west by a tall menhir which can be compared with the Le Manio Giant. After skirting the Kerlescan alignments and moving northwards, visitors will reach the long megalithic chamber with a lateral entrance, protected by its mound (circa 3000 BC), a rare example in this region of a type of collective tomb more frequently found in Northern Germany and Denmark.

Visit of the Le Ménec alignments

Return to the western extremity of Kermario and walk westwards to see, firstly, the eastern end of the Le Ménec alignments, ending in a circular enclosure. Continuing towards the west, visitors cannot fail

to be impressed by the amount of energy required to erect the hundreds of menhirs and by their impact on the landscape. At the western end the aligned stones are taller and, on top of the hill, the enclosure made of standing joined slabs is still visible in spite of the modern houses occupying the area. Seen from this high point the view towards the east of the Le Ménec alignments is spectacular.

Le Manio quadrilateral enclosure.

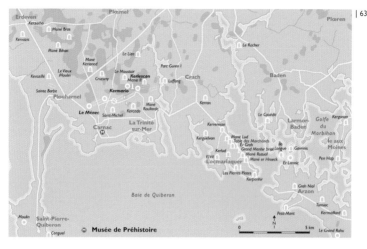

Ⓜ Musée de Préhistoire

Around Carnac: the megalithic context

The wealth of megalithic sites concentrated within a perimeter of a dozen kilometres around Carnac allows the diversity and force of the alignments' context to be appreciated. These fifty or so major sites of the Neolithic period (5th-3rd millennia BC) confer an exceptional sacred character on the region. Four excursions are proposed in the Carnac hinterland – the Quiberon Peninsula, the Locmariaquer region and the Gulf of Morbihan – pinpointed here by their most spectacular monuments.

Locmariaquer and the Grand Menhir Brisé

This site has been equipped in order to explain the results of the recent excavations carried out around the largest (20 m) and heaviest (300 tonnes) menhir of prehistoric times as well as the Er Grah (or Er Vinglé) long barrow and the Table des Marchands dolmen whose head stone with an ogival, probably anthropomorphic, profile is decorated with a repeated crook motif.

The site of Gavrinis

This used to be a hill in the middle of the countryside: in Neolithic times the sea level was 6 metres lower than at present, so the island in the Gulf of Morbihan where it is situated did not exist. To reach it, visitors must take a boat from Larmor Baden. The Gavrinis dolmen is the most richly decorated megalithic monument.

The Petit-Mont site

Situated in the district of Arzon, an enormous mound with stone architecture was in use during the three main megalithic phases in the Morbihan region: the early phase, around 4500 BC, is characterised by the long barrow. The large menhirs with a standing idol 6 metres tall date from the middle period, around 4300 BC; the megalithic chamber tombs, for their part, date from the most recent phase, around 4000 BC. The restoration of this complex architecture gives a good idea of the skills of the Neolithic builders.

Finally, two museums present the offerings or grave goods – vases, ceremonial axes, stone pendants, arrowheads and flint tools – and provide a great deal of information on daily life in Neolithic times: the Musée de Préhistoire at Carnac and the Musée de la Société Polymatique in Vannes.

Gavrinis: under its mound, the long passage tomb presents slabs entirely decorated with motifs including the idol (buckler), the axe, the crook, the bow, the snake and the horn-shaped symbol.

Petit-Mont.

A short bibliography

Bailloud (Gérard), Boujot (Christine), Cassen (Serge), Le Roux (Charles-Tanguy), *Ca:nac. Les premières architectures de pierre,* CNMHS/CNRS éditions, coll. "Patrimoine au présent", Paris, 1995.

Briard (Jacques), *Les Mégalithes de l'Europe atlantique…,* Errance, Paris, 1995.

Giot (Pierre-Roland), L'Helgouach (Jean), Monnier (Jean-Laurent), *Préhistoire de la Bretagne,* Ouest-France, Université, Rennes, 1979.

Le Roux (Charles-Tanguy), *Gavrinis et les îles du Morbihan, les mégalithes du Golfe,* Ministère de la Culture, coll. "Guides archéologiques de la France", Paris, 1985.

L'Helgouach (Jean), *Locmariaquer,* Éditions Jean-Paul Gisserot, Paris, 1994.

Michell (John), *Megalithomania,* London, Thames and Hudson, 1982.

Mohen (Jean-Pierre), *Le Monde des mégalithes,* Casterman, Tournai-Paris, 1989.

Id., *Les Mégalithes, pierres de mémoire,* Découvertes Gallimard, Paris, 1998.

Riskine (Anne-Élisabeth), *Carnac, l'armée de pierres,* Imprimerie nationale, Paris, 1992.

Sellier (Dominique), "La morphologie des menhirs de Kerlescan", *Revue archéologique de l'Ouest,* 1991, pp. 83-97.

Thom (Alexander), Thom (A.-S.), *Megalithic Remains in Britain and Brittany,* Oxford, 1978.

In homage

to Jean L'Helgouach and Jacques Briard, specialists in Armorican megaliths.

Acknowledgements

Charles-Tanguy Le Roux, Gérard Bailloud, Serge Cassen, Christine Boujot, Joël Lecornec, Jean Guilaine, Anne-Élisabeth Riskine, André Cariou, Emmanuel Couet, Raymond Lachat, Annie Fortune.

Captions

Cover photographs

Front: Sunrise over the Kermario alignments
Back: Kermario chamber tomb
Front flap: Anthropomorphic signs picked on a stone in the Pierres Plates tomb, Locmariaquer (detail).

Visit, p. 48

Background: Print from *La Création de l'homme […],* Henri du Cleuziou, 1887.

Drawings and plans

Pol Eger: 36, 41, 51, 58t.
Jean-Pierre Mohen: 44, 58b, 59, 60-61, chronology.

Photographic credits

Arthepot/A.-F. Kersting: 37; Arthepot/P. Salou: 29; bibliothèque municipale, Rennes: 10-11, 12, 14-15; J. Briard: 38c, 47; J.-L. Charmet: 6tl, 9t, 24, 25; CMN, P. Berthé: front cover, 1b, 4, 6t, 6b, 17, 20r, 31b, 33b, 34-35, 38c, 39, 41, 46, 48, 50t, 51, 52, 54, 55b, 57t, 59-60, 62t, 63t1, D. Chenot: 50b, P. Pitrou: 23b, M. Rapilliard: 56t, B. Renoux: 49b, 56b, 57c and b, 62b, 63t2, É. Revault: 57t; musée de Préhistoire, Carnac: 20l, 32t /reprod. Ph. Berthé: 13, 21, 38t; reserved rights: 1c, 5b, 16, 26-27b, 40bl, 42, 43, 45t, 53; éditions d'art Jack, Louannec: 5t; éditions Jos Le Doaré: front flap, 40tr, tl and br, 55t; C. Huyghens: 30; J.-M. Labat: 28c, 32c, 33t; A. Leclaire: 50c; Le Cornec: 63b; Le Doaré archives: 18-19; Médiathèque de l'architecture et du patrimoine, Archives photographiques/reprod. CMN: 1t, 2-3, 8t, 26t, 27t; J.-P. Mohen: 28t, 38b, 61; musée d'Archéologie du Morbihan, Vannes: 22-23t/ Y. Boëlle: 28b /G. Hersant: 32b; L. Robin, Quimper: 7; Roger-Viollet: 8-9b; M. Schaffner: back cover; Scope/Bernard Galeron: 44-45b, 63c.

Centre des monuments nationaux
President
Philippe Bélaval
Managing director
Bénédicte Lefeuvre

Éditions du patrimoine
Publishing director
Jocelyn Bouraly
Publications coordinator
Catherine Donzel
Production coordinator
Carine Merse
Series editor
Alix Sallé

Documentation coordinator
Cécile Niesseron
Translator and copy editor
Ann Sautier-Greening
Graphic design
Atalante/Paris
Layout
Jean-François Gautier
Graphics
Pol Eger
Photoengraving
Scann'Ouest/Saint-Aignan-de-Grand-Lieu
Printing
Néo-Typo/Besançon, France
Dépôt légal: september 2000
Reprinted: 2003, 2006, 2007

Reprinted
IME/Baume-les-Dames, France
2011
Imprimerie Deux-Ponts, Bresson, France
December 2013